W9-BTM-697

Animals with Super Powers
See-Through
Animals

by Natalie Lunis

Consultant: Edith Widder, Ph.D.
CEO, President & Senior Scientist
Ocean Research & Conservation Association, Inc.

BEARPORT
PUBLISHING

New York, New York

Credits

Cover and Title Page, © Doug Weschler/Animals Animals Enterprises and U-photo/Shutterstock; 4T, © Ronald Caswell/
Shutterstock; 4B, © Radius/SuperStock; 5T, © Exactostock/SuperStock; 5B, © Peter Batson/Image Quest Marine; 6, © age
fotostock/SuperStock; 7, © Pere Soler/Flickr/Getty Images; 8, © Michael Fogden/Animals Animals Enterprises; 9, © Heidi
& Hans-Jurgen Koch/Minden Pictures/Getty Images; 10, © imagebroker.net/SuperStock; 11, © Exactostock/SuperStock;
12, © goldenangel/Shutterstock; 13, © Herb Segars/gotosnapshot.com; 14, © Radius/SuperStock; 15, © Flirt/SuperStock;
16, © Peter Batson/Image Quest Marine; 17, © Deepseaphotography.com; 18, © Dr. Richard E. Young; 19, © Solvin Zankl/
SeaPics; 20, © CB2/ZOB/WENN/Newscom; 21, © AFP Photo/Hiroshima University/Newscom; 22T, © James Christensen/
Foto Natura/Minden Pictures; 22M, © Glenn Young/Shutterstock; 22B, © Chris Newbert/Minden Pictures/Getty Images;
23, © U-photo/Shutterstock.

Publisher: Kenn Goin
Editorial Director: Adam Siegel
Creative Director: Spencer Brinker
Design: Dawn Beard Creative
Cover: Kim Jones
Photo Researcher: Picture Perfect Professionals, LLC

Library of Congress Cataloging-in-Publication Data

Lunis, Natalie.
  See-through animals / by Natalie Lunis.
     p. cm. — (Animals with super powers)
  Includes bibliographical references and index.
  ISBN-13: 978-1-61772-120-5 (library binding)
  ISBN-10: 1-61772-120-4 (library binding)
  1. Camouflage (Biology)—Juvenile literature. I. Title.
  QL767.L86 2011
  591.47'2—dc22

                    2010045408

For more information, write to Bearport Publishing Company, Inc., 101 Fifth Avenue, Suite 6R,
New York, New York 10003. Printed in the United States of America in North Mankato, Minnesota.

122010
10810CGF

10 9 8 7 6 5 4 3 2 1

Contents

Now You See Them, Now You Don't!

Some animals look just like the green leaves that surround them. Others are a perfect match for the rough, gray rocks they live among. Still others are colored so that they disappear into the sandy bottom of the sea.

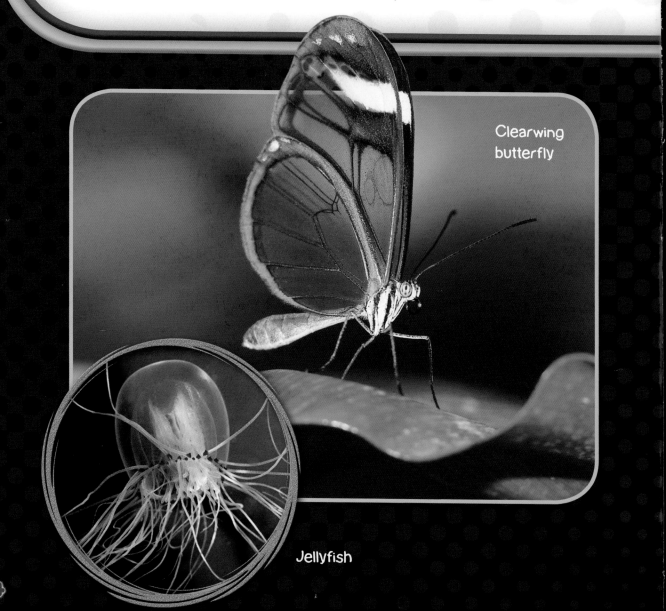

Clearwing butterfly

Jellyfish

There are some creatures, however, that have very little or no color at all. These **transparent**, or see-through, animals are able to **camouflage** themselves by letting their background show through their bodies. In other words, wherever they go, they are just about invisible. In this book, you'll get to see nine of these animals and find out how their invisibility helps them survive. Pay close attention, though—or they might disappear before your eyes!

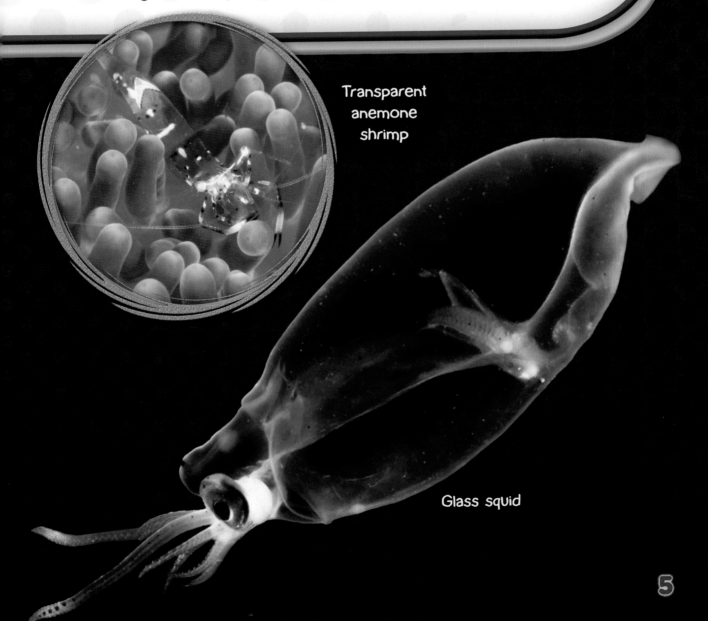

Transparent anemone shrimp

Glass squid

Clearwing Butterfly

Butterflies are some of the most colorful animals on Earth. One kind, however, has wings that have almost no color at all. It is known as the clearwing butterfly.

The butterfly's transparent wings make the **insect** hard to see when it is keeping still. For example, when it is resting on a leaf or sipping the **nectar** that it feeds on from a flower, the clearwing is nearly invisible. The butterfly is also hard to see when it is in flight. That's even more important for its survival, since birds often spot and snatch butterflies as the insects move their wings to flutter through the air.

Clearwing butterflies live in warm, wet forests in Central America.

Clearwing butterflies are also known as glasswing butterflies.

vein

Veins are parts of a butterfly's wings that are not transparent. These narrow tubes carry blood and also help the wings hold their shape.

Glass Frog

What's going on in there? The skin on a glass frog's back and belly are so thin that you can see into its body. Some of the parts that are visible are the bones, heart, **liver**, and **intestines**.

The purpose of the frog's see-through body is not to show off its insides, however. Instead, by allowing the color of the leaves in its forest home to show through, its almost transparent greenish skin helps it hide. The creature has lots of reasons to hide, too. Many kinds of birds, snakes, and lizards also living in the forest like to eat the little frogs.

To stay even safer from enemies, glass frogs move around and look
for food only at night. They hunt flies and other small insects.

The skin on a glass frog's underside is especially thin, allowing the body parts inside to show through clearly.

There are more than a hundred **species**, or kinds, of glass frogs. They live high up in trees in warm, wet forests in Mexico, Central America, and South America.

Transparent Anemone Shrimp

Most people would have a hard time spotting the little transparent shrimp on an animal called a sea anemone (uh-NEM-uh-nee). Fortunately for the shrimp, so do most of the sea creatures swimming by. After all, they can't try to eat what they can't see.

Surprisingly, the shrimp's safe hiding place is full of danger. The anemone's wiggling **tentacles** are covered with tiny poisonous stingers, which the animal uses to attack fish and other **prey**. Why doesn't the anemone sting and eat the little shrimp? Scientists think that the shrimp coats itself with some of the slimy **mucus** that covers the anemone. Once the two animals share the same slime, the anemone pays no attention to its little guest—treating it as if it really were invisible.

A close-up view of a transparent anemone shrimp

transparent
anemone shrimp

The transparent anemone
shrimp got its name because
of the stinging sea creature
that it hides in.

There are many kinds of sea
anemones and tiny transparent
shrimp living together in warm,
shallow ocean waters around
the world.

sea anemone
tentacles

Transparent Sea Butterfly

Most transparent animals live in oceans around the world. However, unlike the transparent anemone shrimp, they do not live in shallow waters. Instead, they live in the **open ocean**.

In these waters, away from land and the ocean floor, there is nothing to see but water. The only way to hide from fish and other **predators** is to look as much like water as possible. That is exactly what the sea butterfly—a kind of transparent sea snail—does. By blending in with the water around it, this see-through creature has a good chance of escaping the attention—as well as the jaws—of any enemy that is nearby.

Many kinds of fish, including mackerel like these, eat sea butterflies— when they can find them.

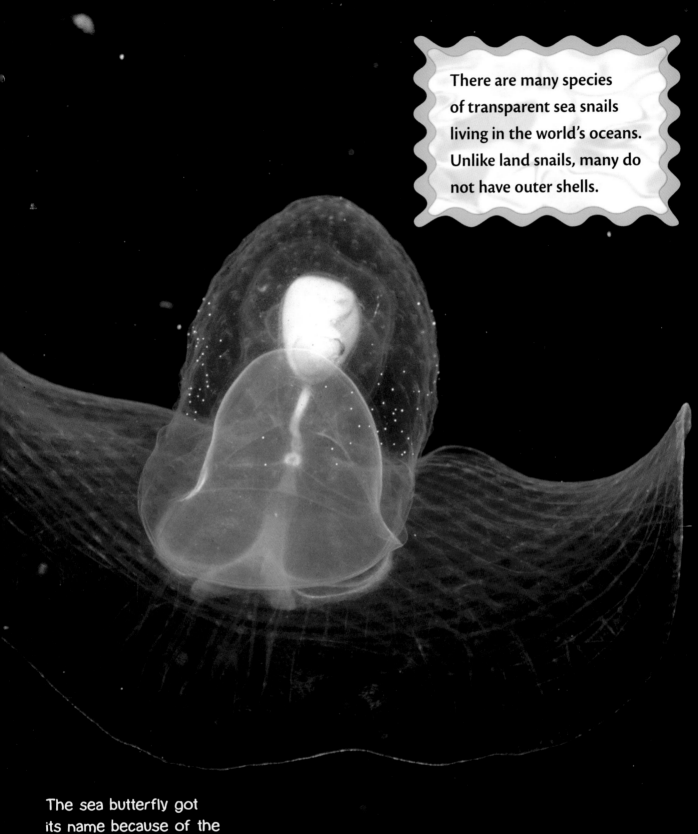

There are many species
of transparent sea snails
living in the world's oceans.
Unlike land snails, many do
not have outer shells.

The sea butterfly got
its name because of the
way it looks as it moves
its wing-like flaps up and
down in order to swim.

Jellyfish

There are more than 1,500 kinds of jellyfish. Some are as small as a grape, and some are as large as a washing machine. All jellyfish, however, are about 95 percent water—and most are almost as clear.

Even though these see-through creatures aren't very meaty, a few kinds of fish, crabs, and turtles hunt them. The jellyfish can't move very fast to escape, so it's a good thing their invisibility helps them hide from these enemies.

Of course, jellyfish have to eat, too. For many kinds, transparency helps with hunting. These jellyfish have long, stinging tentacles. Fish and other sea creatures swim into the tentacles without seeing the rest of the jellyfish. A poison in the tentacles then **paralyzes** the prey, and the jellyfish pulls its meal into its big mouth.

Some jellyfish have tentacles that seem harmless because they look like seaweed. Others have tentacles that act as **bait** because they look like floating fish or shrimp. Still others have tentacles that are nearly invisible.

tentacles

Jellyfish live in all the world's oceans.

Glass Squid

All squids are strong swimmers, and many are fierce hunters. They have eight arms and two tentacles, which they use to grab fish, crabs, and other sea creatures. They also have parrot-like beaks, which they use to tear their prey apart. Glass squids, which is how squids with see-through bodies are known, have an extra advantage—they are nearly invisible in the ocean waters where they live.

The glass-like creatures' near invisibility doesn't just come in handy for hunting, though. It also helps keep them safe from animals that hunt them. That's an important need, since many kinds of fish, whales, and even seabirds like to catch and eat squids.

Glass squids have shorter tentacles than other kinds of squids and are slower swimmers.

There are about 60 species of glass squids. Some, like the one shown here, can roll themselves into a ball when faced with enemies.

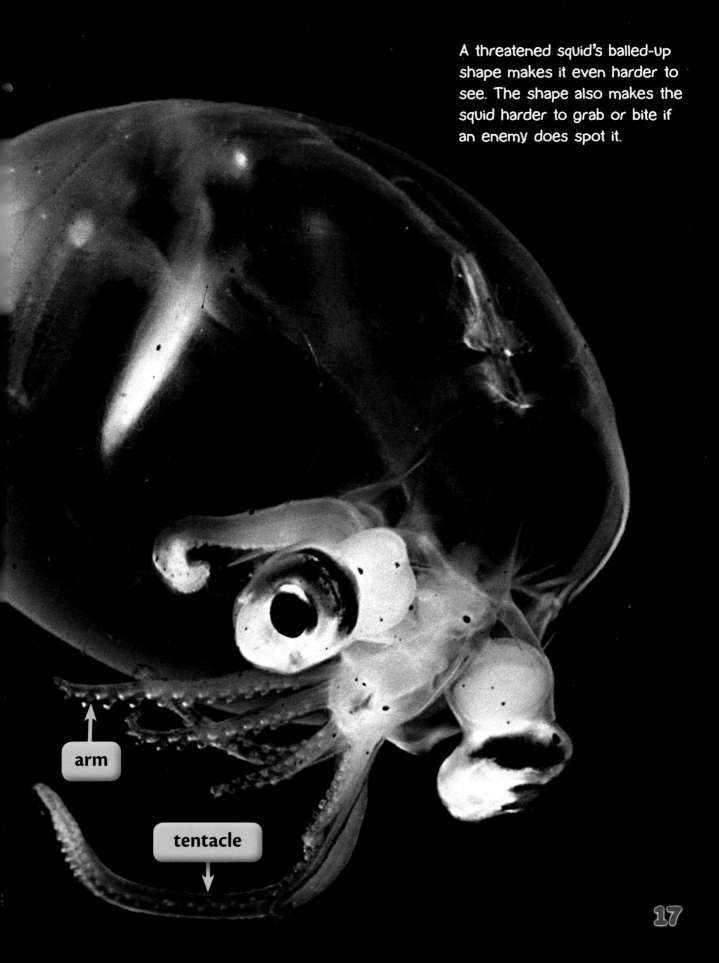

A threatened squid's balled-up shape makes it even harder to see. The shape also makes the squid harder to grab or bite if an enemy does spot it.

arm

tentacle

Transparent Octopus

The transparent octopus has the shape of a spooky Halloween ghost. It is also see-through like a ghost. Because it can get to places and jet away with great speed, it even appears and disappears suddenly—just like a ghost.

Unlike ghosts, however, the transparent octopus is very real. Still, scientists don't know very much about this rarely seen creature. They do know that octopuses hunt some animals and are hunted by others. So it's probably safe to say that its invisibility helps it hide from both predators and prey. It's also clear that not every part of the octopus is transparent—its dark eyes stick out of its head, and several **internal organs** show through its skin.

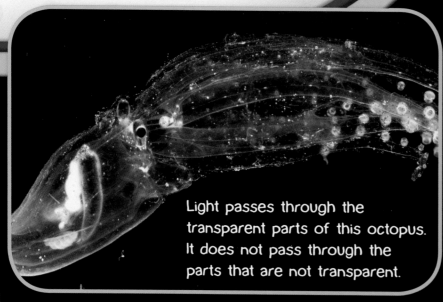

Light passes through the transparent parts of this octopus. It does not pass through the parts that are not transparent.

eye

eye

The transparent octopus, which is also known as the glass octopus, lives in warm ocean waters around the world.

Transparent Zebrafish and Transparent Frog

Surprisingly, some transparent animals don't live in the wild. They are not found in the sea or in forests—or on any kind of land at all. These transparent animals can be found only in scientific **laboratories**.

For example, both the transparent zebrafish and the transparent frog were **bred** by scientists. The scientists raise these animals in order to study them up close. In particular, they want to look inside their bodies and see how their internal organs grow. The scientists also use the transparent animals to learn more about diseases such as cancer and how they develop. So, even if the animals' transparency did not come about to help them survive, it might someday help many people survive and live long lives.

This transparent zebrafish was bred by scientists at Children's Hospital Boston in Massachusetts. Its beating heart can be seen through its skin.

High school students **dissect** dead frogs in science class to learn about the animals' bodies—inside and out. The scientists who bred transparent frogs think that before long, students will be able to observe and study the live see-through frogs instead.

This transparent frog was bred by scientists in Japan.

More About See-Through Animals

- The caterpillars that grow into clearwing butterflies are not transparent. Instead, they are silver-gray.

Glass frog

- Glass frogs are tiny—about the size of a quarter.

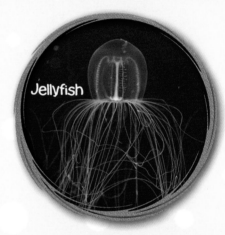

Jellyfish

- Jellyfish are not really fish. They are actually closely related to sea anemones.

Leaf scorpionfish larva

- The larvae (LAR-vee), or young form, of many kinds of sea animals—including many kinds of fish—are transparent. Their transparency gives the helpless young creatures a better chance of avoiding predators.

- Most kinds of jellyfish and glass squids are bioluminescent. That means they have the ability to make light in their bodies.

Glossary

bait (BAYT) food used to attract an animal to a trap

bred (BRED) raised

camouflage (KAM-uh-flahzh) to blend in with one's surroundings because of the colors and markings on one's body

dissect (dye-SEKT) to cut apart an animal in order to study it

insect (IN-sekt) a small animal that has six legs, three main body parts, two antennas, and a hard covering called an exoskeleton

internal organs (in-TUR-nuhl OR-guhnz) body parts, such as the heart, lungs, and stomach, that do particular jobs and are found inside the body

intestines (in-TESS-tinz) the long, tube-shaped parts inside an animal's body where food is turned into useful fuel and waste

laboratories (LAB-ruh-*tor*-eez) places where scientific experiments are carried out

liver (LIV-ur) a large important organ in the body that cleans the blood

mucus (MYOO-kuhss) a sticky liquid made by an animal

nectar (NEK-tur) a sweet liquid made in flowers

open ocean (OH-puhn OH-shuhn) ocean waters that are not near shore or the bottom of the ocean

paralyzes (PA-ruh-*lize*-iz) causes something to be unable to move

predators (PRED-uh-turz) animals that hunt other animals for food

prey (PRAY) animals that are hunted and eaten by other animals

species (SPEE-sheez) groups that animals are divided into, according to similar characteristics; members of the same species can have offspring together

tentacles (TEN-tuh-kuhlz) long, arm-like body parts used by some animals for moving, feeling, or grasping

transparent (trans-PAIR-uhnt) able to let light shine through so that objects that are behind can be seen; another word for *see-through*

Index

Bibliography

Doubleday, Ayla, and James B. Wood (eds.). "Marine Invertebrates of Bermuda: Symbiotic Cleaner Shrimp." (www.thecephalopodpage.org/MarineInvertebrateZoology/Periclimenesanthophilus.html)

Johnsen, Sönke. "Transparent Animals." *Scientific American*. February 2000. (www.biology.duke.edu/johnsenlab/pdfs/pubs/scientificamerican.pdf)

Strugnell, Jan, Mark Norman, Alexei J. Drummond, and Alan Cooper. "Neotenous Origins for Pelagic Octopuses." (www.adelaide.edu.au/acad/publications/papers/Octopus%20Neoteny.pdf)

Read More

Earle, Sylvia A. *Sea Critters*. Washington, D.C.: National Geographic (2006).

Lunis, Natalie. *Box Jellyfish: Killer Tentacles (Afraid of the Water)*. New York: Bearport (2010).

Yaw, Valerie. *Color-Changing Animals (Animals with Super Powers)*. New York: Bearport (2011).

Learn More Online

To learn more about see-through animals, visit
www.bearportpublishing.com/AnimalswithSuperPowers

About the Author

Natalie Lunis has written many science and nature books for children.
She lives in the Hudson River Valley, just north of New York City.